A Curious George® Activity Book

I Am Curious About Safety

Activities by Diane Molleson

Featuring
Margret and H.A. Rey's
Curious George

Illustrations by
Manny Campana

SCHOLASTIC INC.

New York   Toronto   London   Auckland   Sydney

ISBN 0-590-42700-8

Illustrations by Manny Campana

12 11 10 9 8 7 6 5 4 3 2 1   8 9 8 0 1 2 3/9

Printed in the U.S.A.   34
First Scholastic printing, September 1989

This is George.
He lives with the man
with the yellow hat.

George is very curious.
He is curious about you.
Write your name here.

_____

If you are curious about
the answers to the puzzles,
look in the back of the book.

George and the man with the yellow hat are having breakfast.

"I have to run some errands, George," the man said. "Why don't you play outdoors until I come back? Be sure you don't wander too far from the house!"

George is eager to go outside.
But first he has to get dressed properly.
In each of the pictures below, George is missing something important. Draw a line from the picture to the clothes he needs.

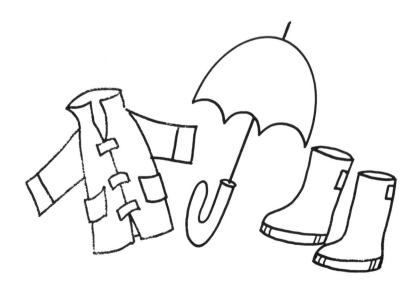

It was a warm, sunny day outside.
George looked around for someplace good to play.

Help George find a safe place to play. In
the picture below, circle the places where
George can play without getting hurt. Put
an X when an area is too dangerous.

Suddenly a kitten ran by.
"That kitten will be fun to play with,"
thought George.
He started to run after the kitten.

Help George cross the street without
getting hurt.
Color the traffic light at the top of the
page green for George.
Color the traffic light on the bottom red.

Oh, no! George is lost!

Many of the paths below lead to danger.
One path will lead George to someone who can
help him.

START

FINISH

The policeman took George to his car to drive him down to the station.

What is the first thing George did when he got in the car?

Unscramble the words in the sentence below
to find out.
The numbers will tell you how.
Print the words on the dotted line.

r g o e e G   t p u   n o   i s h   l e t s a t b e
4 5 3 2 6 1   3 1 2   2 1   2 3 1   7 2 4 1 3 8 5 6

___ _____   ___   __   ___   _____

The police chief was standing
on the steps of the police station when
George and the policeman arrived.

Can you find all the police officers hidden
in this picture?
How many are there?

Inside the station, two police officers were showing some guests the new alarm system.

Color the police officers' uniforms. Color the spaces with a 1 blue, the spaces with a 2 yellow, and the spaces with a 3 black.

George looked around the police station.
He was so curious!

The names of seven things George saw in the
police station are hidden in the word search
puzzle below.
Circle the ones you find.

WORD LIST

policeman	jail	siren	hat
alarm	key	lock	

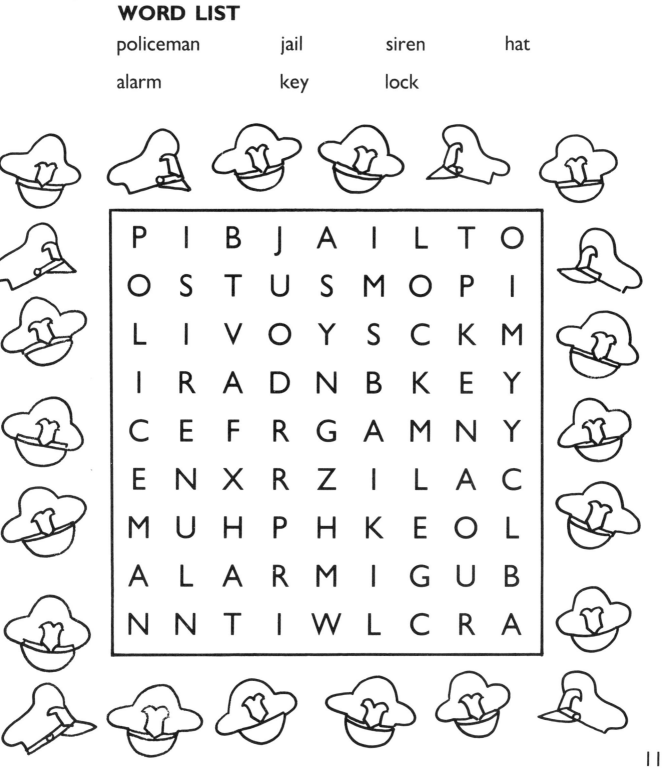

P I B J A I L T O
O S T U S M O P I
L I V O Y S C K M
I R A D N B K E Y
C E F R G A M N Y
E N X R Z I L A C
M U H P H K E O L
A L A R M I G U B
N N T I W L C R A

While the policeman went to make a phone call, George saw a door.
Where did it go?
George opened the door.
It led to the basement, where he saw rows of jail cells.

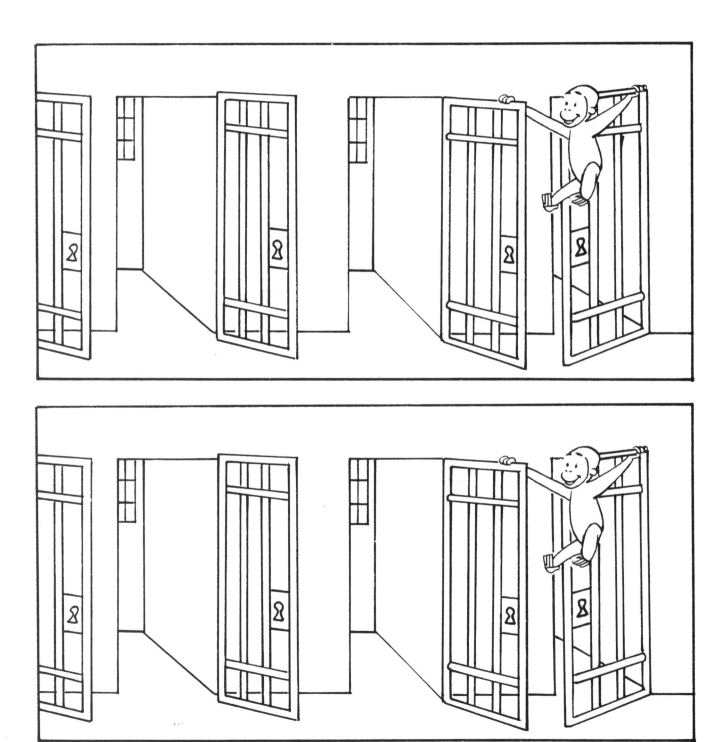

George climbed up on the bars and swung
from cell to cell.
What fun for a little monkey!

On these two pages are pictures of the same
scene.
Which picture is different from the others?
Put a circle around it and color it in.

George was so very busy clanging doors that he did not see someone come down to inspect the cells.

Clang!

Oh, no, who did George lock in jail?

Connect the dots and see.

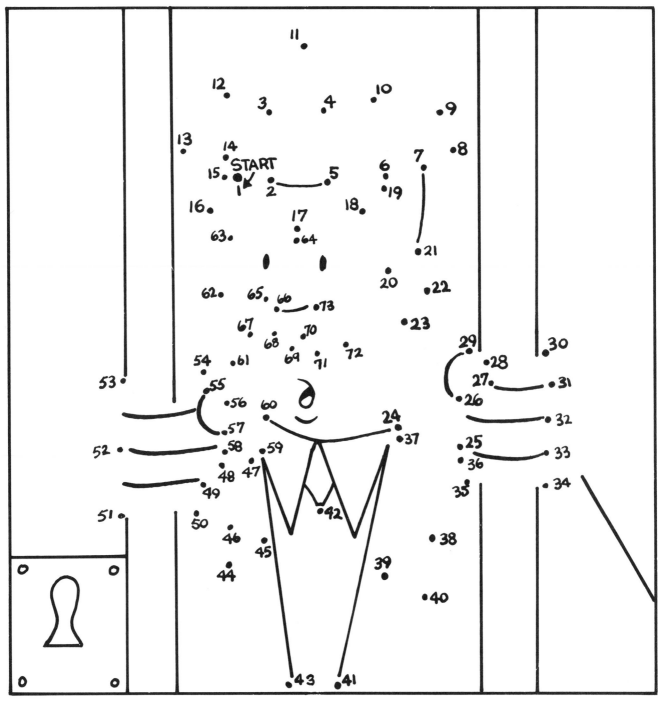

The police chief was very angry.
"GUARDS! Get that monkey!"
he shouted.
But no one heard him, and George ran away.

What does the police chief need to get out of the cell?

To find out, print the names of the pictures below.
Then copy down the letters in the boxes.
(See if you can find the hidden object in the picture.)

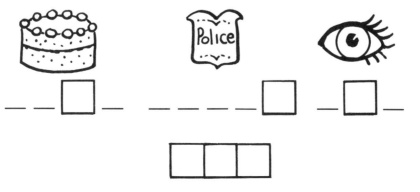

_ _ ☐ _   _ _ _ _ ☐ _☐ _

☐☐☐

George ran by the new alarm system.
He was curious.
What would happen if he pushed
that big, round button?

Draw a circle around the roundest thing in each row.

  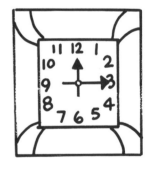

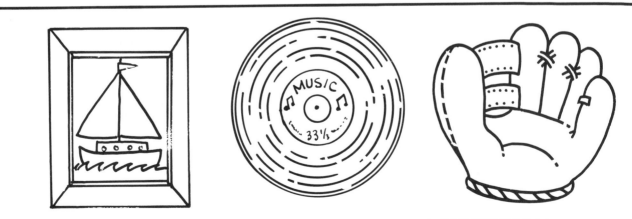

Suddenly, sirens started screaming!
Police came running from every direction.

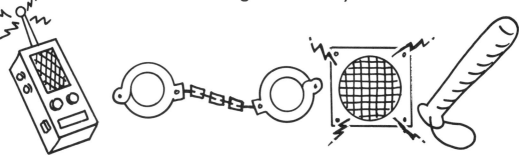

These things are in the picture below.
Color them in when you find them.

"Will someone please get me out of here?"
the chief shouted.
He was very angry.
Then the officer who found George said,
"But chief, this monkey is lost!"
"Lost?" said the chief. "Do you know what
we do with lost monkeys?"

Do you remember what adventures George has
had at the police station so far?
Put the pictures in the right order.

"We give them ice cream!"

These two pictures are almost the same, but not quite.
Circle the things that are different in the bottom picture.

"And then we get them found!"

George learned something that he wants to share with you.
Solve the rebus and see what it is.

20

CURIOUS GEORGE AT THE FIRE STATION

"I have a surprise for you, George," said the man in the yellow hat. "Today we're going to visit the fire station!"

Circle the thing in each row which George must not touch.

21

On their way to the fire station, George and
his friend saw some things that will help
you stay safe if there is a fire.
Color in all the things in this picture
that have to do with fire safety.

The fire chief was very happy to see George
and the man with the yellow hat.
He gave George a fire hat to wear.

Draw a line from each hat
to the person it belongs to.

George looked all around the fire station.
There was so much to see.

Match the pictures with the words in the word list.
Then write the words in the numbered squares.

WORD LIST

pole

engine

hat

fireman

house

bed

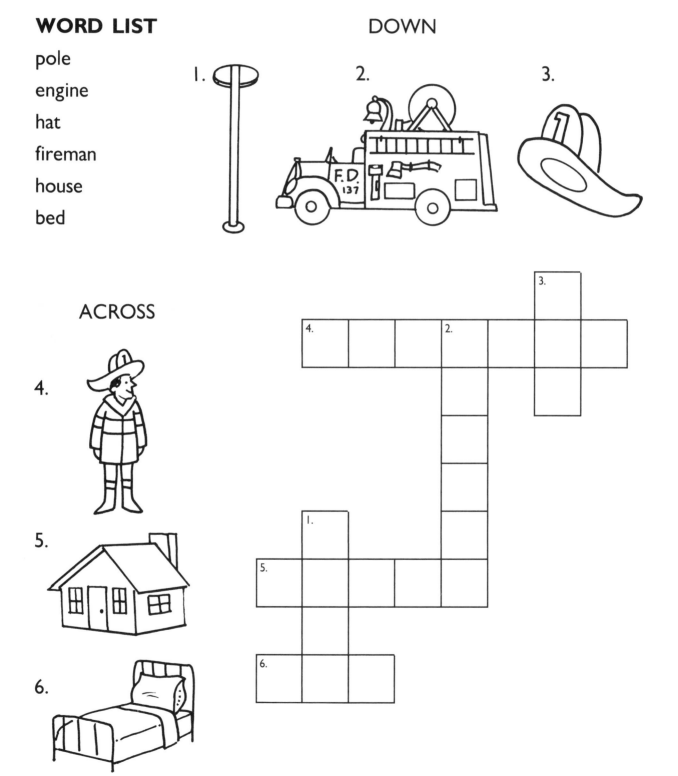

The chief showed George and his friend the fire engines.
What do you see on the fire engine?
Unscramble the words to find out.
The numbers below will help you.

r e d l a d
6 5 4 1 2 3

_ _ _ _ _ _

s o e h
3 2 4 1

_ _ _ _

l e b l
4 2 1 3

_ _ _ _

a g l h i s l h f t
3 8 2 5 7 4 6 9 1 10

_ _ _ _ _ _ _ _ _ _

x a e
2 1 3

_ _ _

25

"We're proud of our fire engines," said the chief.
"We keep them as bright and shiny as we can."
Look very closely at the picture.
Then cover the page.
See how much you can remember.

What did you see?
Color the right picture in each row.

One fireman was polishing a big brass bell on the wall.
"This is our alarm bell," said the chief.
"Whenever it rings, we know there is a fire."
Circle all the things on this page that
ring when people need help.

AMBULANCE

F.D.

POLICE

SMOKE ALARM

The fire engine also had a bell on it.
"We ring that bell on our way to a fire,"
said the chief, "Then people will get
our of our way."

Color the fire truck in the picture.
Color the spaces with a 1 red.
Color the spaces with a 2 black.
Color the spaces with a 3 yellow.
Color the space with a 4 green.

The fire chief taught George what to do if his house caught fire.

GET OUT FAST!

STAY LOW AND GO!

Crawl on your hands and knees.
Stay under the smoke — smoke can kill.

Then the fire chief told George what people should do
if their clothes caught on fire.

STOP

DROP

ROLL

COOL

The fire chief wanted George to meet their fire dog,
Sally, and her puppies.
George put all the puppies in their basket.
"Yip! Yip! Yip!" they barked.
Draw a circle around the fattest puppy.
Draw a square around the longest puppy.
Draw a triangle around the puppy that has
the most spots.

Near the puppies' basket is a big round hole
with a pole in the middle.
When the alarm rings,
the fire fighters slide down the pole
to the fire engines below.

George wants to slide down like a real fire fighter.
How does George get down the pole?
Color the correct picture.

Then George climbed onto the fire engine and sat behind the steering wheel.

Match the different wheels below with the objects they belong to.

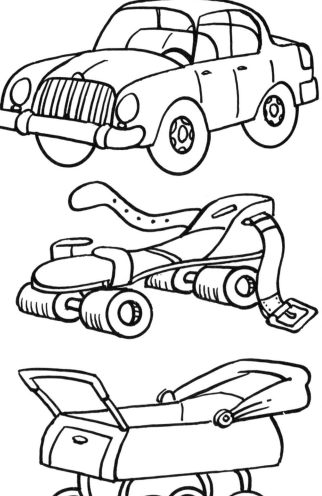

George pretended to be a real fire fighter.
Who would you like to be?
Draw a picture of yourself dressed up as someone,
or something else.

George was curious.
What would happen if he rang the bell?

There are lots of bells in the fire station.
Add up the ones you see below to find out how many there are.

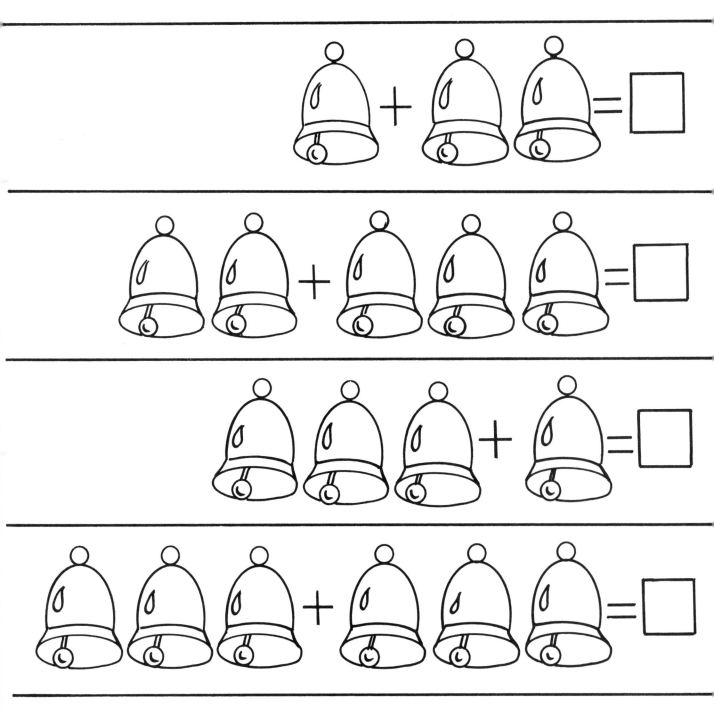

George pulled the string.
Clang! Clang! Clang! went the bell.

In each line, circle the thing that makes the most noise.

The fire fighters all jumped out of bed.
"Fire! Fire! Fire!" they shouted.
F is for fire. Color all the things
that begin with F in this picture.

Quickly the fire fighters put on their uniforms, and slid down the pole.
These fire fighters need help getting dressed.
Draw a line from each fire fighter to the thing
he or she needs.

Help the fire fighter reach the truck.

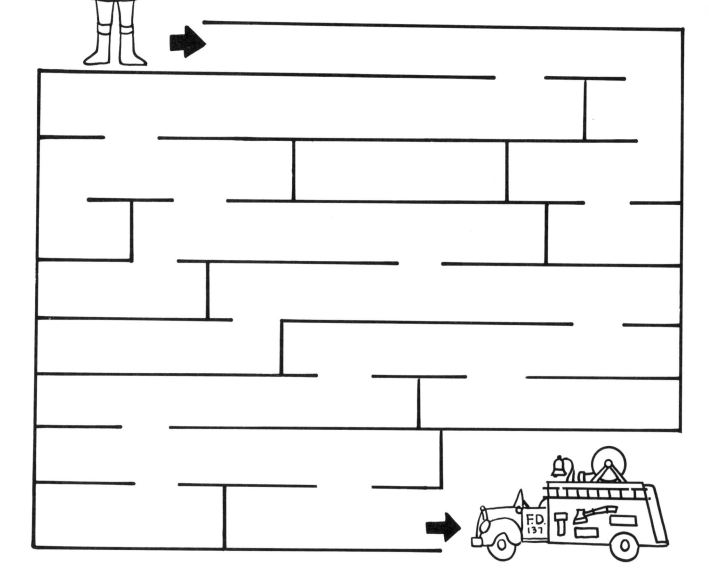

But it was a false alarm.
When the fire fighters got to the engine all they saw was a little monkey.
"George," said the chief, "fighting fires is serious business. You must never use the alarm unless there really is a fire."
George felt terrible.

Just at that moment, one of the puppies got out of its basket.
It wandered over to the edge of the hole and looked down.
One more step and it would fall.
The puppy needs help!

The word help is written six times in the puzzle below.
Can you find all six places?

a e d f g c b e
l h e l p i m a
l e y e l p c r
e l o h e l p d
h p v n g o l h
e d j l e r p e
l n s q y d a l
p a r d h e l p

George knew what to do.
He climbed up the pole
and caught the puppy in his hat!
Sally was very happy her puppy was safe.

Draw a line from each puppy to its mother.

"Three cheers for George!" shouted the fire fighters.
Can you find all the fire fighters hidden in this picture?

The chief made George an honorary fire fighter for saving the puppy.
He also let him keep the hat.
"Come back to visit us anytime," said the chief.
"Good-bye, George," called the fire fighters as
George and the man with the yellow hat left the station to go home.

Color all the pictures you saw in this book.

At home, George and his friend looked for
ways to make their home safe from fire.
Circle the three things in this picture
that are dangerous.

ELECTRIC HEATER

George and his friend had a fire drill.
George knows two ways to leave the house if there is a fire.
Can you find them in the maze below?

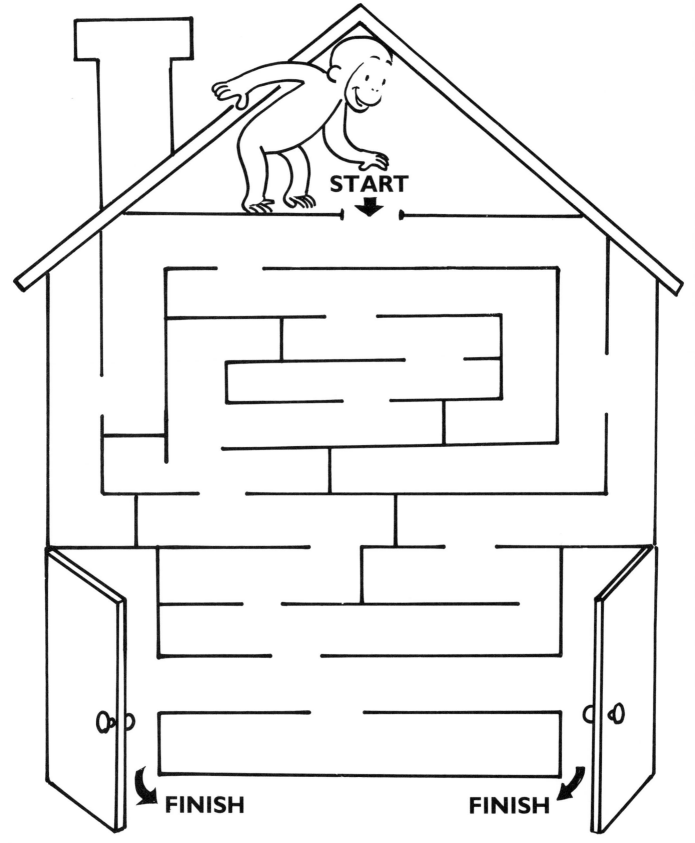

START

FINISH   FINISH

ANSWERS

Page 4

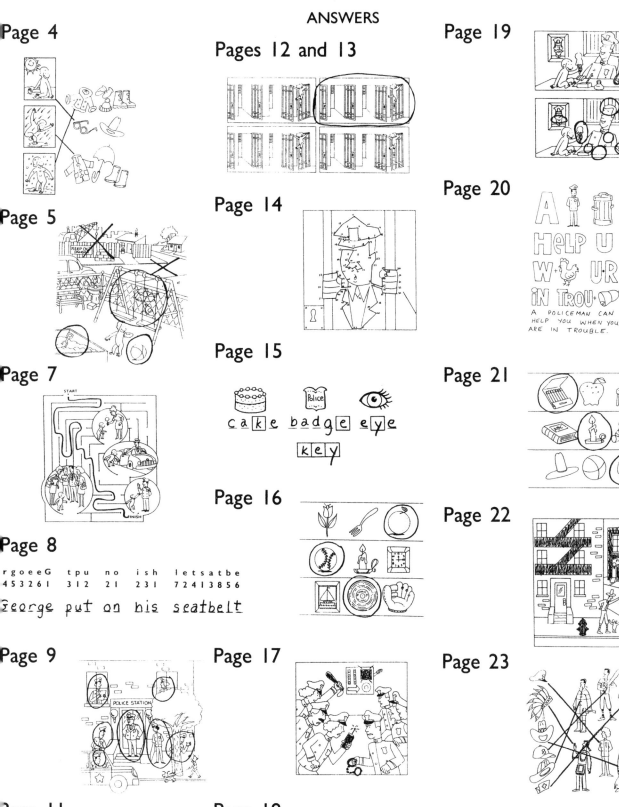

Pages 12 and 13

Page 14

Page 5

Page 15

cake badge eye
key

Page 7

Page 16

Page 8

```
rgoeeG   tpu   no   ish   letsatbe
453261   312   21   231   72413856
```

George put on his seatbelt

Page 9

Page 17

Page 11

Page 18

Page 19

Page 20

A 🚓 🔔
HELP U
W + 🐓 UR
iN TROU + 🔔

A POLICEMAN CAN
HELP YOU WHEN YOU
ARE IN TROUBLE.

Page 21

Page 22

Page 23

Page 24

47

Page 25

redlad
654123

soeh
3241

lebl
4213

ladder   hose   bell

aglhislhft
38257469110

xae
213

flashlight   axe

Page 27

Page 36

Page 42

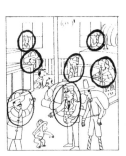

Page 28

Page 37

Page 43

Page 32

Page 38

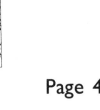

Page 44

Page 33

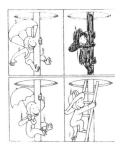

Page 39

Page 45

Page 34

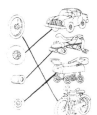

Page 40

Page 41

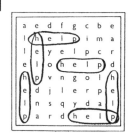

Page 46